A Metal Can

Sarah Ridley

FRANKLIN WATTS
LONDON·SYDNEY

First published in 2006 by
Franklin Watts
338 Euston Road
London NW1 3BH

Franklin Watts Australia
Hachette Children's Books
Level 17/207 Kent Street
Sydney NSW 2000

ISBN: 978 0 7496 6060 4
Dewey Classification: 669

Series editor: Sarah Peutrill
Art director: Jonathan Hair
Design: Jemima Lumley
Photography: Alan Williams
Photo credits: James L. Amos/Corbis: 8tr, 26cl.
Nathan Benn/Corbis: 8bl. Anthony Blake Photo
Library/Alamy: 30tr. Corbis: 24, 27bl. Howard
Davies/Corbis: front cover cl, 6b, 26tl. Dynamic
Graphics/Alamy: 28tr. Chris Fairclough/Franklin Watts: 29.
Goodshoot/Alamy: 25b. John van Hasselt/Sygma/Corbis:
25t, 27tr. K Photos/Alamy: 28b. Ray Moller/Franklin Watts:
30b. Luc Monnet/Sygma/Corbis: 23b. NASA: 31t. Charles
O'Rear/Corbis: 7t. Charles Rotkin/Corbis: 9. Paul A
Souders/Corbis: 7b. Stockbyte Silver/Alamy: 31cr. Hugh
Trefall/Alamy: 28cl. Zefa/Corbis: 5b, 30cl, 31bl. All other
photography by AlanWilliams. Every attempt has been
made to clear copyright. Should there be any inadvertent
omission please apply to the publisher for rectification.

A CIP catalogue record for this book is available from the
British Library.

With thanks to Ball Europe for their help with this book.

Printed in Malaysia

Franklin Watts is a division of Hachette Children's Books.

Contents

4 This can is made from a metal called aluminium.

6 Aluminium comes from a type of rock called bauxite.

8 The aluminium pours into moulds.

10 The reels of aluminium arrive at the can-making factory.

12 The cups pass into the next machine.

14 It is time to print a design on the cans.

16 A machine sprays each can with lacquer.

18 The cans are each given a neck.

20 The cans get a final check.

22 The can ends are made at a different factory.

24 The cans and their ends arrive at the filling factory.

26 How a metal can is made

28 Metal cans

29 Recycling aluminium

30 Other uses for aluminium

32 Word bank

32 Index

This can is made from a metal called aluminium.

Aluminium, like many metals, is found in rocks under the ground. Once it has been removed from the rocks, it becomes a very useful material. It is a solid at room temperature but it can be bent into shapes quite easily.

◀ This drinks can is filled with a soft drink called 'fizz'.

▼ The drinks company can choose from a variety of ring-pull colours.

The can is made by a company that makes cans for various drinks companies. Before work starts, the drinks company decide how the can will look. What will be printed on the can? What colour ring-pull will it have?

Metal cans

Aluminium is used to make drinks cans because it is strong, lightweight, easily bent into shape and it does not rust. Drinks are heavy so the lighter the can containing them the better. Then it is easier to lift and transport them to the shops.

Steel is another metal that can be used to make food and drinks cans. It is also easy to shape but it will rust so steel has to be coated with another metal called tin - giving the name 'tin' can. Many drinks and foods are stored in steel cans - from fizzy drinks to fish, custard to cat food. The design of all drinks cans allows the greatest number of cans to be stacked on a supermarket shelf.

Can you think which foods might be stored in each of these cans?

Aluminium comes from a type of rock called bauxite.

Bauxite is a reddish rock that is mined mainly in Australia, West Africa and the Caribbean.

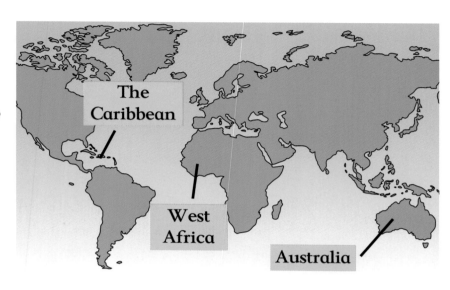

➤ Bauxite is found mainly in three areas of the world.

The Caribbean

West Africa

Australia

Drills or explosives break up the bauxite. Then huge machines load the rocks onto trucks, to begin their journey to the processing factory.

◄ All the soil has to be removed before mining can begin. The mine can stretch over a huge area.

Alumina is a fine white powder.

At the processing factory, the bauxite is treated with chemicals and water until all that is left is a powder, called alumina.

A substance called cryolite is added to the alumina. Huge amounts of electricity are passed through the mixture of alumina and cryolite, which changes it into molten aluminium.

Who discovered aluminium?

Pierre Bertier discovered alumina in bauxite rocks at Les Baux in southern France in 1822. However, it wasn't until 1886 that two chemists, Charles Hall and Paul Heroult, invented the process of removing the alumina from the bauxite. This process is still used today.

This red hot aluminium will harden and turn grey as it cools.

The aluminium pours into moulds.

The molten aluminium is poured into moulds where it hardens to form ingots. It takes four tonnes of bauxite to make one tonne of aluminium.

► A stack of aluminium ingots.

▲ The aluminium ingot glows yellow while it is heated.

Each ingot of aluminium is now changed into thin sheets. At the start, each ingot is 2 metres wide, 8 metres long and 60 centimetres thick. By the end of the process, the ingots will change into thin sheets - still 2 metres wide but only 3 millimetres thick and very long. To make the thin sheets the ingots are first heated to soften the metal.

Then the ingots are passed backwards and forwards through rollers, becoming longer and thinner each time they go through.

When the ingots have been rolled into thin sheets of metal of the correct thickness, they can be wound onto reels. Now they can be loaded onto a truck to leave this factory and travel to the can-making factory.

Huge reels of finished aluminium sheet stacked at the factory.

In the past

Although people have only been using aluminium for about 150 years, other metals have been a part of everyday life for thousands of years. People first discovered that they could use fire to extract metals from particular rocks about 10,000 years ago.

Gradually people experimented with different metals to make a variety of objects, from weapons to jewellery. Some of these metal objects have been discovered by archaeologists. Look in your local museum to see what has been found in your area.

The reels of aluminium arrive at the can-making factory.

This can-making factory never sleeps! Its machines keep working all day and all night, making about six million cans a day. First the workers fix a reel of sheet aluminium onto a machine called a press. The shiny sheet of aluminium is coated with a thin layer of oil, to make it move smoothly, before going into the press.

▲ The huge reel feeds into the press machine.

Inside, the press stamps out several wide shallow dishes, called cups. The cups come out of the other end of the machine on a conveyor belt.

▼ An aluminium cup.

◀ The cups stick to a conveyor belt by suction.

Why recycle aluminium?

Millions of cans of drink are opened each day across the world. Aluminium is a great material to use for cans because it is very easy to recycle. Once it has been cleaned up, it can be used over and over again. This reduces the demand for new aluminium to be extracted from bauxite, leaving more in the earth for people who might need it in the future. For more about how to recycle aluminium cans, see page 29.

For more about how to recycle aluminium cans, see page 29.

Look on the side of some cans - do they have a recycling sign like this picture?

The cups pass into the next machine.

The cups go into the ironing machine and are pushed by a punch through a set of rings until they are the correct length. This is called 'ironing'. At the same time the bottom of each cup is made into a curved shape. The machines work at great speed.

▶ The cans leave the ironing and trimming machine.

The cans go back onto the conveyor belt again. At the next stage, a machine with a sharp blade trims each can to the correct size.

◀ The conveyor belts carry the cans between the different machines.

◀ The can is now a long cylinder shape.

Now a different machine washes and rinses the cans with hot water and chemicals to remove any traces of oil. The cans move along on a metal wire conveyor belt, and pass through huge ovens that dry them.

In the past

Before fridges, freezers and cans existed, people found other ways of preserving food for those times of the year when there was less fresh food available. Packing food in salt stopped it from going rotten, as did pickling food in barrels full of water, salt and vinegar. Hanging some meat or fish over a smoking fire had the same effect. Many foods were dried in the sun, like raisins, dates, wheat and rice. Using sugar to make jam meant that people could taste the flavour of summer fruits in the depths of the winter. Many of these methods are still used today.

◀ The clean, dry cans leave the washing and drying machine.

It is time to print a design on the cans.

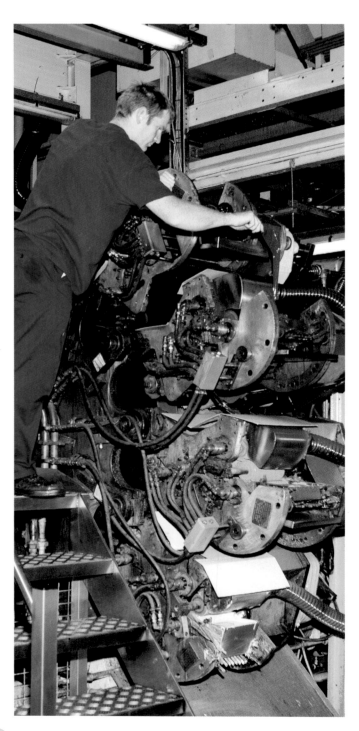

The cans go into the decorating machine. They are decorated with three ink colours - red, yellow and white.

A computer controls how much of each colour is rolled onto a rubber blanket, to make up the correct design. Then each can rolls across the rubber blanket, picking up the ink as it does so. A layer of a material called varnish is then rolled over the ink. This protects the cans and gives them a nice shine.

◁ A worker climbs the steps to fill the machine with the red ink.

The cans then enter a machine that dries the ink and the varnish.

➤ The decorated cans coming out of the drying machine.

The drinks company wants to show a lot of information on the outside of the can. The strong design and colours will attract the shopper. Information about the ingredients of the drink, where it was made and how to recycle it are shown on the back.

➤ The can has all its writing and colour now.

In the past

In 1795 a man called Nicholas Appert discovered that food could be preserved by heating it in a sealed container. Then in 1810 Peter Durand invented the metal can. At first, only about 60 cans could be made in one day but gradually people invented faster and faster methods. Now millions of cans are made each day. However, it wasn't until 1935 that a US brewer invented the flat-topped drinks can as we know it now.

A machine sprays each can with lacquer.

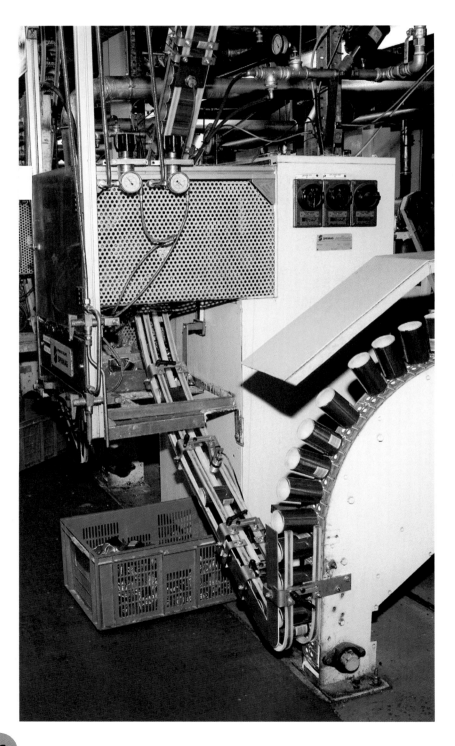

Each can has to be coated on the inside with lacquer. This is a special coating that prevents the metal mixing with the contents of the can.

On the cans go again, into another oven where the lacquer dries. The cans are almost finished now.

◀ Cans enter the lacquer machine at the top (top left of the photograph), are sprayed and then leave at the bottom.

At almost every stage, the machines check the cans for quality. If they are not quite right, they fall into the reject basket. Then they are sent back to the beginning of the process to be recycled.

▲ Rejected cans await collection.

In the past

Early on, some canned food was sealed with lead. This may have caused the strange disappearance of the Franklin Expedition. In 1845, Sir John Franklin set off on a voyage to discover the North-West Passage. He took two boats and 134 men and he made sure that the boats were carrying all the latest equipment, including about 8,000 cans of tinned food.

Time passed and nothing was heard. What had happened to them all? The bodies of just three sailors were found, buried on an island. All had high levels of lead in their bodies, suggesting this was the cause of death. Some scientists now think that the lead sealant in the tin cans must have mixed with the food and so entered the bodies of the sailors, eventually killing them. Perhaps all the members of the expedition died the same way.

The cans are each given a neck.

The cans just need to be pulled in at the top to form the neck of the can. A machine presses each can to make this shape.

▶ Inside this machine, the neck is formed.

◀ The can is finished, all except for its end.

It has taken just a few minutes for the flat sheet of aluminium to be transformed into thousands of cans. Each machine does its job, linked together by many conveyor belts, snaking across the factory.

◀ The cans follow each other around the factory.

➤ From cup to almost finished can in a few minutes.

Why aluminium?

Aluminium is a lightweight, strong, flexible metal that can be made even stronger by mixing it with another metal or another material. It is then called an aluminium alloy. Different alloys are used for different purposes. For instance, copper is added to aluminium to create duralumin - used to build aircraft. Magnesium and magnese are sometimes added to the aluminium in cans. This makes the aluminium stronger but only very slightly heavier.

The cans get a final check.

The final check involves shining light through the cans. This will pick up any tiny cracks or holes. As before the machine automatically rejects any damaged cans.

All the perfect cans are packed in layers and placed on pallets. They are ready to be sent to the filling factory.

Cans rejected at the final stage.

In the past

Shops used to sell all drinks in glass bottles. Glass bottles are easy to clean and reuse, or recycle by melting down the glass and starting again. However, glass is quite heavy and breaks when dropped. Now we can often choose whether to buy our drink in a glass bottle, a plastic bottle or a metal can.

1. The cans go onto a wide conveyor belt. A machine packs the cans into honeycomb-like layers, which will be separated by layers of cardboard.

2. Stacks of cans move into the warehouse on a pallet.

3. Towering stacks of cans fill the warehouse.

4. A fork-lift driver loads the cans, ready for a lorry.

The can ends are made at a different factory.

A reel of sheet aluminium feeds into a machine. Inside, it stamps out thousands of ends every minute. At the same time, it curls the edges and adds a sealant, which will help make the end join tightly to the can.

▲ The aluminium sheet feeds into the end-making machine.

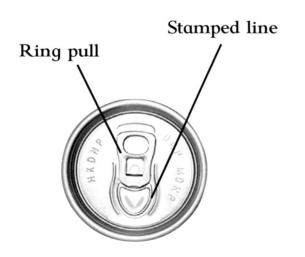

Ring pull

Stamped line

▲ The ends now look like this.

To finish the can end, it needs a ring-pull. This is stamped out of a narrow strip of aluminium and joined to the end. To make the can easy to open, a line is stamped or pressed in the metal so that it will break open with pressure.

All the ends are packed together in paper sleeves and sent off to the filling factory, where the soft drink will be added.

◄ Thousands of ends are packed together in brown paper.

Opening cans

When food cans were first invented (see page 15) people had to hammer them open! Then, in 1858 the first can-opener was invented, and an even better one was invented in 1870. It was much easier to open cans. People also found that it was possible to attach a key to the top and peel back the lid of the can. In 1959, the pop-top can was invented, using a ring-pull and a weakened area to literally pull an opening in the top of the can. More recently cans have tabs that can be pushed into the can. This is so there is no ring-pull to throw away to create litter.

Some cans, particularly ones to store fish, still have a key to remove the top.

The cans and their ends arrive at the filling factory.

A huge number of each can sets off on conveyor belts around the factory to be filled. At this stage, it is extremely important that everything is kept very clean so that no bacteria get inside the cans or the drinks.

▼All the workers in the drinks factory wear hats and overalls to keep the factory clean.

First the machines clean the cans by spraying air and water on them. Then the next machine fills up to 2,000 cans a minute with drink, before a final machine attaches the can ends to the filled cans.

To keep the canned drinks fresh, the cans and the drinks inside are heated for long enough to kill any bacteria that might exist. That way the drinks will stay fresh.

▲ A worker in the drinks factory makes a final check.

A code and 'best before' date is printed on each can. Finally the drinks cans are ready to be packed, sold to shops and drunk.

▲ Within 60 days, these used cans can be recycled and reformed and be back in the shops!

Food poisoning!

Unfortunately, in the past, canned food has been known to kill. If the food inside the cans isn't heated for long enough at the correct temperature, it is possible for deadly bacteria to survive inside. When this happens the people who eat the food get terrible food poisoning, which can lead to death. This happens very rarely today.

How a metal can is made

1. Bauxite, containing alumina, is dug out of the ground.

2. At a processing factory, machines extract the alumina from the bauxite and turn it into pure aluminium ingots.

3. Machines roll the ingots until they turn into long sheets of aluminium.

4. At the can-making factory, a press stamps out aluminium cups.

5. The cups enter another machine where the sides are stretched to form the can shape.

6. After a thorough clean, the cans are printed with a design and dried. Spray guns coat the cans with varnish.

7. The next machine shapes the neck of each can.

11. The cans are heated to kill any bacteria in the drinks. Each can is checked.

8. The cans are stored in the warehouse until they are needed.

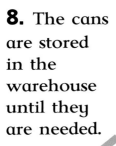

12. The drinks cans are loaded onto lorries, sold to shops and bought by customers.

9. The can ends are made at a different factory.

10. The cans and ends arrive at the filling factory where the cans are filled with drink and closed.

fizz

Metal cans

Huge numbers of aluminium and steel drinks cans are made each year. Cans are also put to other uses.

◄ 'Tin' cans are used to store all sorts of fruit and vegetables in water or syrup, baked beans, custard, tuna fish and pet food.

▲ Beauty products, such as hairspray and deodorant, and some medicines are sold in cans.

► Tennis balls are sold in air-tight cans. This helps to keep them bouncy.

◄ Household products, like paint, are sold in cans as are many other household and cleaning products.

Recycling aluminium

Up to half of all the aluminium in use today will be recycled. It is very easy to recycle and use it over and over again. This includes aluminium cans, food packaging, aluminium foil and the aluminium in cars, lorries and aeroplanes.

➤ Aluminium cans at a recycling centre.

Some more reasons to recycle your aluminium

1. Extracting aluminium from bauxite is difficult and uses a lot of energy. Recycling existing aluminium means much less energy is used, which cuts down on the production of damaging greenhouse gases.

2. Mining bauxite leaves huge scars in the landscape. Even though mining companies keep the original soil and try to restore the landscape when the mining is finished, many animals, plants and insects die.

3. Finally, by keeping aluminium cans out of your other rubbish, it reduces the amount of rubbish that will end up in landfill sites.

What you can do

At home, you can help by recycling all aluminium packaging. Wash out the cans or foil and place them in a box or bag ready for collection. In some places you will need to take your aluminium to a recycling centre.

Sometimes, it is important to separate steel and aluminium cans. Steel cans stick to a magnet while aluminium cans do not. Use a magnet to sort your cans.

Other uses for aluminium

Aluminium is used to make huge numbers of drinks cans. But the fact that aluminium is both strong and light makes it a suitable material for many other uses.

➤ Aluminium can be rolled out into extremely thin sheets, called foil, to wrap around food to keep it fresh. It is also used by cooks to seal food that is cooking.

◀ The lids on yoghurt pots are often made from aluminium, as are many take-away or ready-to-cook meal containers.

▼ Like many metals, aluminium lets heat pass through it easily, making it good to use for cooking pans. The fact that it is a light metal also makes it attractive for large pans that could become very heavy.

Aluminium is used to build space rockets. These rockets need to be extremely strong but also as light as possible so less fuel will be needed to launch them into space, which saves money.

Aluminium can be made into wire. This is used in many ways, including in cables and even to wrap the gut strings of violins.

Aluminium does not rust, unlike some other metals like steel and iron. This makes it a useful material for window frames that will get wet.

Word bank

Bacteria The name for many different types of small single-celled living things that live everywhere. Many are harmless, others help our body to work well but some make us ill if they get inside our body.

Conveyor belt A moving belt or band used to transport goods or objects around a factory.

Ingot The word used to describe a bar of solid metal.

Ironing machine A machine that pulls aluminium cups into a cylinder shape.

Lacquer A liquid that dries to coat a metal or wood.

Landfill site A huge hole in the ground used for storing waste.

Molten A material that is so hot that it has melted into a runny liquid.

Processing factory A factory where the rock, bauxite, is crushed, heated and mixed with chemicals to extract the aluminium from the rock.

Rust Some metals, especially iron, develop a red-coloured substance on them when they get wet. This rust makes the metal weaker.

Suction The act of sucking all the air out of a space. This makes the cups stick to the conveyor belt, even though they are going up in the air.

Varnish A substance very similar to lacquer.

Index

aluminium,
   discovery 7
   history of 7
   qualities 4, 5, 19
   making 7
   recycling 11
   uses 30, 31

bauxite 6, 7, 11, 29

can,
   checking 17, 20, 24

can (continued),
   coating 14, 16
   decorating 14, 15
   ends 22, 23, 24
   filling 24
   heating 25
   history of 15
   ironing 12
   opening 22, 23
   press 10, 11
   stacking 21
   uses 5, 28

food poisoning 17, 25
Franklin expedition 17

mining 6, 29
moulds 8

preserving food 13, 15

recycling 11, 21, 29

steel cans 5, 28, 29